A Robbie Reader

Meet Our New Student From
JAPAN

Lori McManus

Mitchell Lane

PUBLISHERS
P.O. Box 196
Hockessin, Delaware 19707
Visit us on the web: www.mitchelllane.com
Comments? email us: mitchelllane@mitchelllane.com

Mitchell Lane

Meet Our New Student From

Australia • China • Colombia • Great Britain
• Haiti • India • Israel • **Japan** • Korea • Malaysia •
Mali • Mexico • New Zealand • Nicaragua • Nigeria
• Quebec • South Africa • Tanzania • Zambia •
Going to School Around the World

Library of Congress Cataloging-in-Publication Data

McManus, Lori.
 Meet our new student from Japan / By Lori McManus.
  p. cm. — (Robbie Reader: meet our new student from ...)
 Includes bibliographical references and index.
 ISBN 978-1-58415-780-9 (library bound)
 1. Japan—Juvenile literature. I. Title.
 DS806.M323 2010
 952—dc22

                                   2009027336

Printing   1   2   3   4   5   6   7   8   9

                                          PLB

CONTENTS

Japan

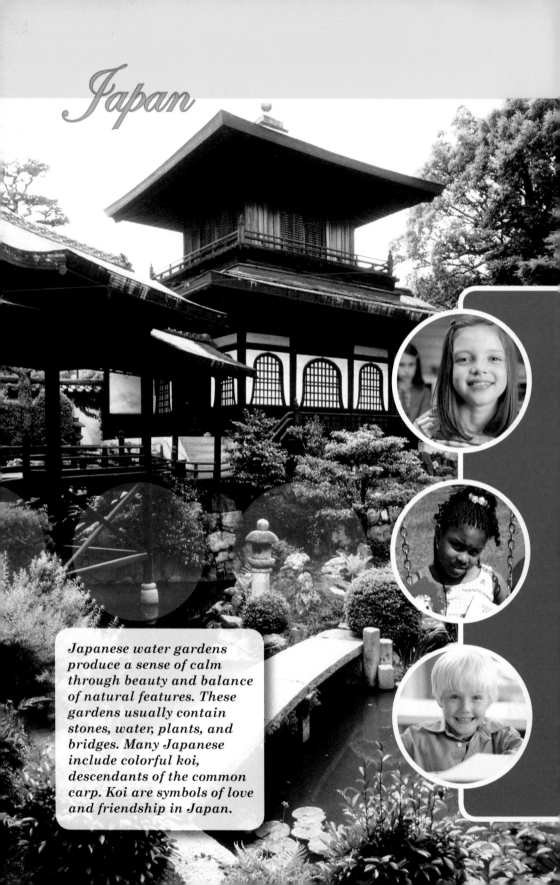

Japanese water gardens produce a sense of calm through beauty and balance of natural features. These gardens usually contain stones, water, plants, and bridges. Many Japanese include colorful koi, descendants of the common carp. Koi are symbols of love and friendship in Japan.

A New Student In Class

Chapter **1**

Allison and her classmates clapped and cheered. Their teacher, Mrs. Gibbs, had just shared the exciting news that a new student from Japan would soon be joining their third-grade class at Mountain View Elementary School. Many questions raced through Allison's mind. Where is Japan? What kinds of games do children play there? What do Japanese people like to eat?

"Our new student's name is Sakura Yamamoto," Mrs. Gibbs announced. Allison listened closely to the new student's name. She heard the sounds *sah-KOO-rah YAH-mah-moh-toh*. Mrs. Gibbs continued, "Sakura is eight years old. She is from Tokyo, a large city along the coast of Japan."

Allison raised her hand and asked, "Does Sakura speak English?"

Mrs. Gibbs replied, "Sakura understands many English words and phrases because she has learned them in school. However, she usually speaks

Where in the World

Sapporo

Hokkaido

Akita

Shirakawa Go

Sea of Japan

Hiroshima

Honshu

Tokyo

Yellow
Sea

Shikoku

Mt. Fuji

Kyushu

Nagasaki

Philippine
Sea

Kyoto

East
China
Sea

Nansei
Islands
(Okinawa)

**Pacific
Oce**

Ryukyu Islands

Bonin Islands

Daito-Shoto

Volcano Islands

FACTS ABOUT JAPAN

Japan Total Area:
147,355 square miles (377,915
square kilometers; slightly smaller
than California)

Population:
127,078,679 (July 2009 est.)

Capital City:
Tokyo

Monetary Unit:
Yen

Religions:
Shinto, Buddhism

Language:
Japanese

Chief Exports:
electronics, cars, ships, computers,
office machines, chemicals

Japanese. You will be able to help her become comfortable speaking in English." She smiled at the students' eager faces. Then she asked the class if they had any ideas for how to make Sakura feel welcome.

Joey said, "We can hang up a Japanese flag!"

Rosa jumped in. "We can make posters that show pictures of Japan."

Allison added excitedly, "Maybe we can learn a few Japanese words."

The Japanese Flag

Mrs. Gibbs summarized the students' suggestions. "Let's gather information about Japan so that we can display pictures and signs that will be familiar to Sakura."

"Can we also learn about the schools in Japan?" Anna asked.

"Of course," said Mrs. Gibbs. "Let's start by finding Japan on a map. Here we are in Ventura." Mrs. Gibbs pointed to a spot along the coast of Southern California close to Los Angeles. Then she used her finger to trace a path on the map as she spoke. "If we travel west across the Pacific Ocean until we are near the continent of Asia, the first large island we'll reach belongs to the country of Japan."

"Japan doesn't touch any of the other countries that are nearby," Sam noticed.

"You're right, Sam," said Mrs. Gibbs. "Japan is made up of islands. The Japanese eat a lot of fish and other sea animals."

"Isn't Mount Fuji in Japan?" Allison asked.

Mrs. Gibbs answered, "Yes, Allison. In fact, much of Japan is covered by mountains. Most people live

Shirakawa Go is a small, old-style village in Japan. The houses have slanted roofs to prevent snow from piling up during the winter. These houses are bigger than the ones found in cities.

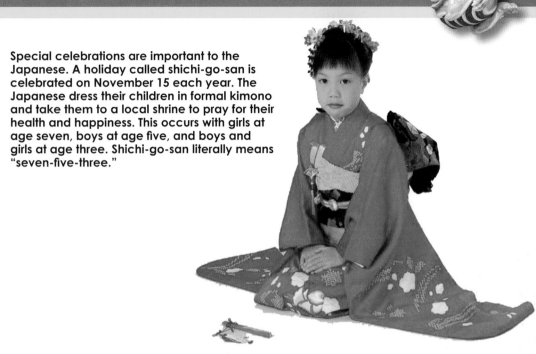

Special celebrations are important to the Japanese. A holiday called shichi-go-san is celebrated on November 15 each year. The Japanese dress their children in formal kimono and take them to a local shrine to pray for their health and happiness. This occurs with girls at age seven, boys at age five, and boys and girls at age three. Shichi-go-san literally means "seven-five-three."

in large cities that have been built on the small amount of land that is fairly flat."

"What are their houses like?" asked Tommy.

"So many fantastic questions!" exclaimed Mrs. Gibbs. "For now, I will tell you that most homes in Japan are small because of limited space. I'd like each of you to write down at least two questions you have about Japan. Over the next week, we will use the Internet and the school library to investigate the answers. By the end of the week, we will be ready to make those welcome signs based on the information we've learned."

At recess, Allison and her friends wondered aloud about the country of Japan. They couldn't wait to meet their new classmate Sakura!

Japan

The bullet train, or shinkansen, *was first used for transportation during the Tokyo Olympics in 1964. Today, bullet trains are a popular way to travel quickly throughout the main island of Honshu.*

Ancient and Modern

Chapter

The country of Japan is very modern. The Japanese travel on the **shinkansen**, or bullet train—one of the fastest trains in the world. They produce some of the finest computers and cars anywhere. Yet many customs and beliefs in Japan have been passed down from ancient times. Japan's national sport, **sumo**, is a type of wrestling that has been practiced for over a thousand years. Many Japanese continue to follow **Shinto**, an ancient religion that honors nature. Since the Japanese value both modern life and ancient traditions, Japan has been called "a land of contrasts."

The first people to live in Japan came from the mainland of Asia around 12,000 years ago. They survived by fishing, hunting, and gathering plants. By 300 BCE, a new group of people, the Yayoi, began to move from Korea and China to Japan. The Yayoi were farmers who knew how to grow rice in flooded fields. They also wove cloth, used bronze and iron to

Sumo is a Japanese form of wrestling in which a contestant loses if he is forced out of the ring or if any part of his body besides his feet touches the ground. Many of the wrestlers weigh over 300 pounds.

make tools, and lived in permanent farming villages.

Eventually, Japan was divided into many provinces (PRAH-vint-ses), or local areas, each ruled by a **clan** or tribe. Around 400 CE, the people who lived on the Yamato Plain became the most powerful clan in Japan. The Yamato clan organized a central government with an emperor and a court system. During this time, the Japanese accepted the

Buddhist religion and the sayings of Confucius, a Chinese thinker who encouraged people to be respectful, generous, and loyal. They also began to use the Chinese system of writing to express ideas in the Japanese language.

In 794 CE, a permanent capital city was built at Heian (modern Kyoto). At that time, the Japanese also stopped trying to copy Chinese customs. Instead, they developed a unique culture that included poems, stories, and plays written in katakana, a Japanese alphabet.

Japan was ruled by an emperor with a central government until 1185 CE. Although the country still had an emperor after that time, the real power belonged to the military leader who protected the emperor. This military leader was called the **shogun**. Soldiers selected by the shogun governed the provinces. The ruling warriors, called **samurai**, valued courage and loyalty. They were excellent at sword fighting and martial (MAR-shul) arts.

A Samurai on horseback

By the late 1800s, Tokyo had become the capital city of Japan. Although many buildings were constructed in Tokyo, the Japanese still saved space for fish ponds and gardens. Many Japanese gardens then and now contain rounded bridges, which add beauty to the gardens.

In 1868, the last shogun turned his power over to the emperor. The government was moved to Edo, which was renamed Tokyo. The emperor's administrators made many changes to help Japan become modern. The changes included creating banks and building railroads and factories. This period was called the Meiji era, after Emperor Meiji.

In the late 1800s, Japan became a powerful country by winning wars against China and Russia. The Japanese military wanted to expand control

over other Asian nations. The United States disagreed with Japanese expansion, so the country stopped selling oil to Japan. Without this oil, the Japanese military would lose their power in Asia.

To keep control as long as possible, the Japanese attacked a U.S. navy base in Pearl Harbor, Hawaii, in 1941. After this attack, the United States entered World War II to fight against Japan and other

Emperor Hirohito (front row, center) posed with officers of the Japanese Imperial Navy. At the beginning of World War II, the Japanese Imperial Navy was the third largest navy in the world and well known for its powerful torpedoes, large submarines, and excellence at night-fighting.

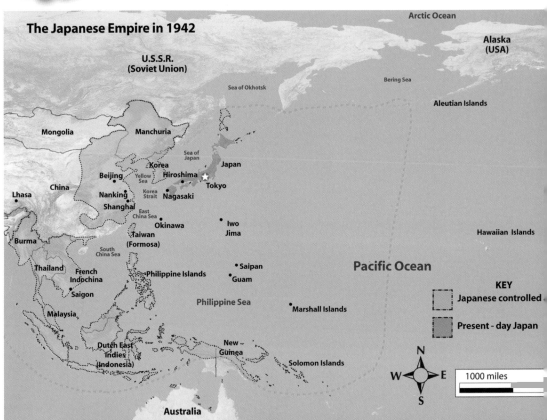

The Japanese Empire in 1942

Arctic Ocean

Alaska (USA)

U.S.S.R. (Soviet Union)

Sea of Okhotsk

Bering Sea

Aleutian Islands

Mongolia

Manchuria

Sea of Japan

Japan

Korea

Hiroshima

Beijing

Yellow Sea

Tokyo

China

Nanking

Korea Strait

Nagasaki

Lhasa

Shanghai

East China Sea

Hawaiian Islands

Okinawa

Iwo Jima

Burma

Taiwan (Formosa)

South China Sea

Pacific Ocean

Thailand

French Indochina

Philippine Islands

Saipan

Guam

KEY

Saigon

Philippine Sea

Japanese controlled

Malaysia

Marshall Islands

Present - day Japan

Dutch East Indies (Indonesia)

New Guinea

Solomon Islands

N

W   E

1000 miles

S

Australia

By the 1930s, Japan's government began using military force to create a Japanese Empire. By 1942, the Japanese Empire reached its largest size, extending into many countries in East Asia. Some of the Asian countries were glad at first that Japan freed them from control by European countries. However, the conquered Asian countries did not like the Japanese government's proud attitude. Several of these countries fought against Japan in World War II to stop the invasions and control. The Japanese finally withdrew from other countries after surrendering in August 1945, an action that brought World War II to an end.

Today, Tokyo is a busy, wealthy city. Most major Japanese companies have their head office in one of Tokyo's business districts. Japan's main government buildings and the Emperor's Palace are also in Tokyo.

enemies. After many battles, the United States dropped two atomic bombs on Japan, one on Hiroshima and the other on Nagasaki. These bombs killed many Japanese people and forced the government of Japan to surrender.

After the war, Japan established a new type of government based on the American system of elections. Japan received money from other countries to help rebuild its businesses and schools. Today, Japan is a strong country known for making excellent cell phones, cameras, and cars.

Japan

Natural beauty abounds in this nation of islands. Given the easy access to water, the Japanese enjoy sports such as kayaking, swimming, snorkeling, and surfing. The mountains provide the Japanese with opportunities for snow skiing, rock climbing, hiking, and mountain biking.

A Country of Islands

Chapter 3

Every spring, people in northern Japan ice-skate outdoors and ski on snowy mountains. At the same time, others are swimming in the ocean along the warm, sunny shores of the islands in southern Japan. These differences in **climate** exist because of Japan's length. The country stretches 1,860 miles (3,000 kilometers). That is about the distance from Maine to Florida. The farther north a person travels in Japan, the colder the weather gets.

Japan is an **archipelago**, or string of islands. The amount of land on all the islands combined is about equal to the size of California. The four main islands of Japan are Hokkaido, Honshu, Shikoku, and Kyushu. Honshu is the largest. Nearly 4,000 smaller islands are also part of the country. In Japan, the beach is a popular place to relax. Since the country is narrow, everyone can get to the beach within a few hours.

The weather in Japan is usually warm. The average daily temperature is 80 degrees Fahrenheit. However, the northern coast of Honshu and the island of Hokkaido have very cold winters that bring heavy snow. The cold comes from icy winds that blow from Siberia. The northwestern coast of Honshu is known as the Snow Coast. Few people live there. In contrast, the eastern coast of Honshu contains large, crowded cities. Tokyo, the capital of Japan, is located on this coast.

Japan gets a lot of rain. Most islands receive at least 60 inches of rain per year. About 75 percent of the rain falls between June and September, the "rainy season." Although the rain is important for crops such as rice and wheat, Japan usually

A farmer plants rice in a flooded area called a paddy field. Rice is a major crop in Japan.

Tsunami, created by Katsushika Hokusai between 1823 and 1829. Hokusai used a style of wood block printing called *ukiyo-e*. He painted many natural features of Japan.

experiences five or six **typhoons** each year. These storms bring very heavy rain and strong winds. They sometimes cause damage to buildings, farms, and roads.

Japan experiences as many as 1,500 **earthquakes** per year. Minor earthquakes occur almost daily somewhere in the country. Major earthquakes occur infrequently, but can cause severe damage. When an earthquake occurs under the ocean floor, the vibrations may cause a **tsunami**, the Japanese term for tidal wave.

Mount Fuji is the tallest and most sacred mountain in Japan. On clear days, Mount Fuji is visible from over 90 miles away, but it is often surrounded by clouds. The Japanese are proud of Mount Fuji and feel it represents the beauty and strength of their country.

Almost 75 percent of Japan is covered by mountains, including at least 40 active **volcanoes**. The mountains contain many beautiful natural features such as waterfalls, rivers, forests, and hot springs. Monkeys, bears, deer, and flying squirrels live in the forests. The highest mountain in Japan, Mount Fuji, is located on the island of Honshu. Mount Fuji stands 12,388 feet tall. It is a volcano, but it has not erupted for over 300 years.

The red-crowned crane is a symbol of peace, luck, and longevity in Japan.

Since Japan has such a small amount of land flat enough for building cities or farming, people have changed some of the landscape over the years. By building **dikes** to keep the water out, some bays and rivers have been turned into land areas. Some mountains have been carved and flattened to provide places for growing rice or building homes. In spite of these human-made changes, Japan is still a country of great natural beauty.

Japan

Osaka Castle, first built in 1583, sits in the modern city of Osaka. Before it was a castle, it served as sleeping quarters for monks and as a fort for protection against samurai warriors. It was rebuilt several times, most recently in 1931. It is now a museum.

Life in
Japan

Chapter 4

Most Japanese people dress in Western clothes and live modern lives that include cell phones, movies, computers, and visits to amusement parks. Baseball is a very popular sport in Japan. Professional baseball games are shown live on television. The Japanese also enjoy karaoke. Karaoke shops provide customers with rooms where they can sing with their friends in private. Some traditional hobbies include *taiko*, or Japanese drumming, and origami, art created by folding paper.

The Japanese are educated and practical. Yet ancient traditions and values still exist in Japan. The Japanese are known for their order, cooperation, respect for elders, and self-discipline. These qualities are important in a crowded country of over 127 million people.

Most Japanese accept both the religions of **Buddhism** and Shinto. Typically, Japanese get married at a Shinto **shrine** and are buried in a

The Shinto wedding ceremony takes place in a shrine with only close family members present. Afterward, the couple welcomes a larger group of guests at another location. The bride typically changes her clothing two or three times during the reception, including at least two *kimono* and one Western style dress.

Buddhist-style funeral. For these formal occasions, both men and women wear the traditional kimono, a robe made of decorative fabric, and an obi, a belt also made out of fabric. Most Japanese have a small Buddhist altar inside their home to honor and remember their ancestors. A small number of Japanese have accepted Christianity and other religions.

The Japanese celebrate many national holidays. The New Year celebration takes place from January 1 to 3 each year. It is the most important holiday in Japan. Families place special decorations such as pine branches and sacred straw ropes around the house. Children receive gifts of money,

Buddhist temples consist of a number of buildings organized around a courtyard. The main hall houses images and statues of the Buddha. Worshipers face these images and pray with their palms pressed together. Another important structure, the pagoda, symbolizes the Buddha's tomb.

Top: The Japanese dress formally for special celebrations or jobs. Geishas, trained female entertainers, apply thick white makeup and red lipstick to their faces. A little girl wears a kimono during the Otsu Festival in the fall.

Below: Taiko means "drum" in Japanese. The large drum used by this *taiko* group is made of one solid piece of wood from a 1,200-year-old tree. It is 9 feet 8 inches (294 cm) across in the center and 6 feet 5 inches (195 cm) at the ends, and weighs about three tons.

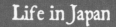

The emperor's birthday is a national holiday in Japan. On December 23, thousands of well wishers enter the gates of the Imperial Palace to wave Japanese flags at Emperor Akihito and his family. The date of the holiday changes with each new emperor.

and adults exchange presents. Most Japanese visit Shinto shrines to pray for success in the new year. The Japanese eat New Year fish and vegetable dishes called *osechi*. Each *osechi* ingredient has a special meaning, like happiness, long life, or health.

Japanese meals consist mostly of rice, fish, and vegetables. Popular vegetables include turnips, carrots, cabbage, cucumbers, and edamame (green soy beans). Meals are served in many small plates and bowls rather than on one main plate. A person may use six dishes for just one meal. The Japanese use chopsticks to pick up solid foods like shrimp and salad. They often drink soup right from the bowl. Many Japanese shop in markets that specialize in one type of food, like a fish market. However, supermarkets do exist in Japan. The Japanese pay for their food and other services with a form of money called yen.

Japanese people follow certain rules when they enter a house. They leave their shoes at the door. Only indoor slippers or socks are worn inside. This keeps the home clean and protects the **tatami**, Japanese carpet made from woven grass. Most Japanese kneel or sit on cushions at low tables to eat their meals. They sleep on **futons**, or firm mattresses, that are laid on the floor at night. During the day, the futons are rolled up so that the space can be used for other activities.

Children in Japan go to school for twelve years, much like children in the United States. Students study common subjects like math, reading, and science, but they also study special subjects like **calligraphy** and Japanese

A monk practices calligraphy.

Salmon-onion sushi. A popular food in Japan, sushi is typically made with seasoned rice, dried seaweed, and a topping or filling such as raw fish. The art of cutting bamboo and leaves to decorate *sushi* bowls is part of the sushi chef's craft.

Japanese foods are served on separate plates so that their individual flavors and appearances can be appreciated. Each person gets his or her own set of chopsticks, bowls, and plates.

The Japanese use two different alphabets plus a system of **ideograms** to write their language. The ideograms, called *kanji*, are pictures or symbols that represent ideas or things rather than sounds. By the time a student finishes sixth grade, he or she has memorized the two alphabets plus over 800 kanji.

poetry. Most schools require students to wear uniforms. Many students take extra classes after school in sports, music, drama, cooking, and study skills. Teachers do not assign homework in Japan.

Japanese children have a recess break in the morning. They go outside to play games like baseball and basketball. Most of their playgrounds also have climbing structures, swings, and seesaws. Japanese children use

Each year, high school baseball teams compete in two annual nationwide tournaments. Large numbers of excited students and parents travel from their hometowns to cheer for their local teams.

"rock-paper-scissors" (*jan-ken-pon*) to decide who will go first in sports and games. They must learn how to play together and work out their own problems on the playground. There is no adult supervision during recess.

Japan

Sakura feels comfortable wearing a uniform to school. In Japan, she also wore a hat during physical education and a bandana when cleaning her school after lunch.

Ohayo Gozaimasu, *Sakura!*

Chapter

Mrs. Gibbs' classroom was ready. Allison and her classmates had made posters that now hung from the ceiling. The posters showed photographs of Mount Fuji, the armor of a samurai warrior, and the **torii** gate of a Shinto shrine. The students had also created colorful *koi-nobori* (koy-noh-BOH-ree) to decorate the bulletin boards. They made a sign that read, *Ohayo gozaimasu, Sakura!* Allison and her friends had practiced saying these words, which mean "Good morning" in Japanese. The words sounded like *OH-hah-yoh go-ZY-moss.* The class had learned a few other Japanese words as well:

ENGLISH	JAPANESE
Greetings	Konnichiwa (koh-nee-chee-WAH)
Goodbye	Sayonara (sah-YOH-nah-rah)
Please	Dozo (DOH-zoh)
Thank you	Arigato (ah-ree-GAH-toh)
Yes	Hai (HY)

"That *osumashi* smells good," said Allison, taking a whiff of the soup they had simmering at the back of the class.

"I can't wait to try some," said Joey.

When Sakura entered the classroom, Allison and her classmates shouted, "*Ohayo gozaimasu, Sakura!* Welcome to California!"

A smile spread across Sakura's face. She bowed to her classmates and her new teacher, which is the Japanese way of greeting with respect. Then she tried out the English she had been practicing. "Good morning. I am glad to be here."

Allison and her friends clapped for Sakura and invited her to join them in eating the *osumashi*. Sakura smiled as she drank the soup and spoke again in English. "It is good!"

Sakura had brought a gift for the class. It was a **bonsai**, a miniature potted tree that had been trimmed to look like it was growing in nature. The children had learned about the Japanese people's strong appreciation for nature.

A bonsai shaped in the informal upright style

Japanese rock gardens, also called Zen gardens, use gravel or sand to symbolize the ripples of water in a lake or sea. Raking the gravel into a pattern takes strong concentration and focus. Stones and shrubs are used to represent other natural landforms like mountains or islands.

The Japanese macaque, also known as the snow monkey, spends most of its time in forests. Unlike most animals, these monkeys often wash their food in water before eating. Macaques also bathe together in hot springs and roll snowballs for fun.

Japanese families often do not have the space for large gardens. Instead, they carefully arrange rocks, gravel, and bonsai to imitate the shapes in nature, like the path of a stream or a waterfall. Mrs. Gibbs and the class realized what a special gift Sakura had given them. The children smiled and said thank you. A few even shouted, "*Arigato, Sakura!*"

At recess that day, Allison and her friends showed Sakura the playground, including the climbing structures, the basketball courts, and the soccer field. Sakura opened her eyes wide and said, "It is big!" She laughed and joined her new friends in the game Red Rover. Sakura already knew the rules

because she played it in Japan, and she learned the English words quickly.

After lunch, Sakura was surprised to find that students in America did not help with cleaning the school. In Japan, all students spend about 20 minutes sweeping floors, scrubbing water fountains, and cleaning the bathrooms. Allison explained with words and motions that in the United States, children get to play again after lunch. The cleaning is done by adults who work for the school.

Japanese students clean their school thoroughly at the end of the school year. They do not grumble at this task because they accept cleaning as part of their normal responsibilities.

Allison and her friends learned how to fold origami cranes during art class that day. While they folded, the teacher read *Sadako and the Thousand Paper Cranes*, a story about a Japanese girl who folded nearly 1,000 origami cranes, hoping her wish to get well would be granted.

At the end of the day, Sakura again bowed to her teacher and classmates. Allison made sure she told Sakura *sayonara* before she left the classroom.

Allison skipped all the way home, thinking about the wonderful new friend she had made. There was so much to learn about Japan from Sakura, and so much she was eager to share about life in the United States. Allison could not wait for tomorrow!

Recipe

How To Make

Osumashi
(Basic Clear Soup)

You will need an adult to help you with this recipe.

Instructions

1. With the help of an adult, use the knife and cutting board to slice mushrooms about ¼ inch thick.

2. Chop a few leaves of chives or the ends of 1 to 2 spring onions.

3. In a saucepan, bring the water to a boil.

4. Stir in dashinomoto, salt, and soy sauce.

5. Remove the soup from heat immediately.

6. Ladle soup into 4 small bowls and garnish each with a mushroom slice and a pinch of chives or watercress.

Things You Will Need

An adult to help you

Cutting board

Knife

Stove

Saucepan

Serving spoon or ladle

4 small bowls

4 soup spoons

Ingredients

1–2 mushrooms

Chives (or the green leaves of a spring onion) or watercress

3 cups water

1 heaping teaspoon dashinomoto

½ teaspoon salt

½ teaspoon soy sauce

Make Your Own
Koi-Nobori

You Will Need

Chenille stems

String

Scissors

Crepe paper streamers

Stapler

Wrapping paper

Clear tape

Every year on May 5, Japanese families celebrate Children's Day by flying fish-shaped wind socks called *koi-nobori*. *Koi-nobori* means "flying carp," a fish known for its strength. Parents tie one *koi-nobori* for each child to a pole in front of their home. As the wind blows, the *koi-nobori* look like they are swimming in water. The wind socks represent a wish for children to be healthy and strong.

Instructions for Making a Koi-Nobori

1. Fold the wrapping paper piece in half lengthwise.

2. Cut out a fish shape without cutting along the folded edge.

3. Staple or tape together the long, open edge of the fish shape.

4. Open the fish shape so that it looks like a wind sock.

5. Bend the chenille stem into a circle that fits the "mouth" of the *koi-nobori*. Staple or tape the chenille stem to the inside of the wrapping paper at the mouth end.

6. Staple or tape 3 or 4 crepe paper streamers to the tail of the wind sock.

7. Staple or tape the string to the mouth end of the fish.

8. Tie the *koi-nobori* to a pole or hold it by the string and run with it.

Further Reading

Books

Imoto, Yoko. *Best-Loved Children's Songs from Japan*. Torrance, CA: Heian International, Inc., 2008.

Messager, Alexandre. *We Live in Japan*. New York: Abrams Books for Young Readers, 2007.

Phillips, Charles. *Japan*. Washington, D.C.: National Geographic, 2007.

Temko, Florence. *Traditional Crafts from Japan*. Minneapolis, MN: Lerner Publications, 2001.

Japanese Tales

Atangan, Patrick. *The Yellow Jar: Two Tales from Japanese Tradition*. New York: NBM Publishing, 2003.

Gershator, Phyllis. *Sky Sweeper*. New York: Farrar, Straus and Giroux, 2007.

Sakade, Florence. *Japanese Children's Favorite Stories*. Boston: Tuttle Publishing, 2003.

Say, Allen. *Kamishibai Man*. Boston: Houghton Mifflin Company, 2005.

Works Consulted

This book is based largely on author Lori McManus' personal experiences and research during a 2004 study visit to Japan sponsored by the Fulbright Memorial Fund Teacher Program. During her time in Japan, the author interacted with many Japanese government officials, subject matter experts, teachers, and families. Other works consulted are listed below.

Central Intelligence Agency: The World Factbook—Japan https://www.cia.gov/library/publications/the-world-factbook/geos/JA.html

Dahlby, Tracy. "Fuji: Japan's Sacred Summit (Except When It's Not)." *National Geographic*. August 2002, pp. 26–45.

Dahlby, Tracy. "Tokyo Bay." *National Geographic*. October 2002, pp. 32–57.

Japanese Characters. Tokyo, Japan: JTB Corp., 2003.

Kamachi, Noriko. *Culture and Customs of Japan*. Westport, CT: Greenwood Press, 1999.

Further Reading

Library of Congress: Country Studies—Japan
http://memory.loc.gov/frd/cs/jptoc.html
A *Look Into Japan*. Tokyo, Japan: JTB Corp., 2002.

On the Internet
Here and There Japan: Snapshots of Life in Japan
http://www.hereandtherejapan.org
Kids Web Japan
http://web-japan.org/kidsweb/
National Geographic: Japan Country Facts, Information, Photos,
Videos
http://kids.nationalgeographic.com/Places/Find/Japan

Embassy
Embassy of Japan in the United States of America
2520 Massachusetts Avenue NW
Washington, DC 2008
Phone: 202-238-6700 (Main)
202-238-6900 (Japan Information & Cultural Center)
URL: http://www.us.emb-japan.go.jp/english/html/index.html
Email: jicc@embjapan.org

Japan 5000 Yen and 1000 Yen notes

1 Yen coin (left) and
50 Yen Coin (right)

PHOTO CREDITS: pp. 3, 28 (top right), 30, 31, 32, 40—Chris Gladis; pp. 4, 19, 22, 25—JupiterImages; p. 6—Richard Lapsley; pp. 14, 15, 21, 35—Library of Congress; p. 17—Mr. Ullmi; p. 24—Ukiyoe; p. 27—David Rich; p. 28—Ewan Cross; p. 29—Junko Kimura/Getty Images; p. 34—Monashee Frantz /Getty Images; p. 48—Lori McManus. All other images—Creative Commons. Every effort has been made to locate all copyright holders of material used in this book. If any errors or omissions have occurred, corrections will be made in future editions of the book.

Glossary

Italics indicate a Japanese word.

archipelago (ar-kuh–PEH-luh-goh)—A group or chain of islands.

bonsai (bon-ZY)—A dwarf-size potted plant or tree that is cut into an artistic shape.

Buddhism (BOO-dih-zum)—A religion of eastern and central Asia focusing on being free from suffering.

calligraphy (kah-LIH-gruh-fee)—An artistic style of writing using a brush and black ink.

clan—A family or group of people who share a common ancestor.

climate (KLY-mut)—The normal weather conditions of a place.

dike—A carefully formed hill of earth built to hold back water.

earthquake (URTH-kwayk)—A shaking or trembling of the earth's crust.

futon (FOO-tahn)—A mattress used on the floor.

ideogram (IH-dee-oh-gram)—A picture or symbol in a system of writing that represents an idea or thing but not a particular word or phrase for it.

kanji (KAHN-jee)—A Japanese system of writing that uses symbols to represent ideas.

samurai (SAM-ur-eye)—The class of ruling warriors in Japan from 1185 to 1868 CE.

shinkansen (SHIN-kahn-sun)—The "bullet train" in Japan that travels up to 190 miles per hour.

Shinto (SHIN-toh)—The ancient religion of Japan that honors nature and the emperor.

shogun (SHOH-gun)—One of a line of military governors that ruled Japan from 1185 to 1868 CE.

shrine—A place where people honor a god, goddess, or other holy being.

sumo (SOO-moh)—A Japanese form of wrestling in which a contestant loses if he is forced out of the ring or if any part of his body besides his feet touches the ground.

tatami (tah-TAH-mee)—Straw matting used as a floor covering in a Japanese home.

torii (TOR-ee)—A Japanese gateway commonly built on the pathway leading to a Shinto shrine.

tsunami (soo-NAH-mee)—A great sea wave produced by an underwater earthquake or volcanic eruption.

typhoon (ty-FOON)—A hurricane that occurs in the eastern region of Asia.

volcano (vol-KAY-noh)—A mountain made of lava that erupted from beneath the earth's crust.

Index

ABOUT THE AUTHOR

Lori McManus spends her days teaching language arts to elementary and middle school students. While earning a master's degree in education, Lori visited Japan with a group of 200 teachers to study Japanese culture and education. She lives with her husband in Ventura, California, where she enjoys the ocean breeze every day.